# GOLD LEAF APPLICATION

## AND

# ANTIQUE RESTORATION

W9-BUE-260

### Ellen Becker

Schiffer Publishing Ltd

4880 Lower Valley Road, Atglen, PA 19310 USA

# DEDICATION

I would like to dedicate this book to my granddaughter, Alexandria, who began learning to gild at the ripe old age of 7. If she can gild, you can gild.

# ACKNOWLEDGEMENTS

A special thanks to my dear friend Tina Skinner, who encouraged me to put this teaching book together for many people to learn by. I'd like to also thank Mary and Pye Chamberlayne, Joan and Ken Benjamin, and Mr. and Mrs. Pierre Olney for allowing me to use their precious pieces for this project. Thanks for the support of Bob Toft. I want to acknowledge my family—my daughter Laura, my son-in-law, Barry, my granddaughter Alexandria, and my son David—who have been tremendous supporters in my life. A special thanks to all of my friends who supported me through this project.

*Designed by Laurie A. Smucker*
Type set in Times New Roman/University Roman Bd BT

ISBN: 0-7643-0632-4
Printed in China

Published by Schiffer Publishing Ltd.
4880 Lower Valley Road
Atglen, PA 19310
Phone: (610) 593-1777; Fax: (610) 593-2002
E-mail: Schifferbk@aol.com
Please write for a free catalog.
This book may be purchased from the publisher.
Please include $3.95 for shipping.

In Europe, Schiffer books are distributed by
Bushwood Books
6 Marksbury Avenue
Kew Gardens
Surrey TW9 4JF England
Phone: 44 (0) 181 392-8585; Fax: 44 (0) 181 392-9876
E-mail: Bushwd@aol.com
Please try your bookstore first.

We are interested in hearing from authors with book ideas on related subjects.

# CONTENTS

# INTRODUCTION

Gold can be beaten into a sheet so thin that it will waft across a room on a single puff of air. Yet it can be affixed to an object—a frame, a box, a chair—and be burnished to a luster that, if cared for, will never fade

Gold leafing or gilding has been around since man first started civilizing the planet. Ancient examples of the gilding craft encircle the globe, from the fertile Nile River basin to the Great Wall of China, and throughout Europe.

So how could an art so ancient, and so widespread, have come as close to extinction as it is today? Indeed, even the essence of the art of has been forgotten by all but the most knowledgeable antique and art dealers. The modern consumer gets gold-colored paint, waxes, or other imitation materials that often cause more harm than good in restoration work, not to mention a counterfeit finish that quickly tarnishes.

Years and years of experience went into the development of gold leafing techniques. The ancient temples, palaces, and tombs of Egypt and Asia are festooned with gilded murals and furnishings. Likewise, the sculptures and architectural edifices left to us by the ancient Greeks and Romans are embellished with gold leafing, as is the art of the Middle Ages, and the holy books hand-written by recluse monks in European monasteries. In the 19th Century in France and England, gold leaf furnishings were essential to the upper-class home, and in America, when the White House was rebuilt after being burnt by the British in 1814, much of the new furniture was gold-leafed in France. Likewise, both wealthy and middle-class Americans wanted to copy the presidential style and the possession of fine gold-leafed furnishings became a mark of distinction.

How could an art once so prevalent have been lost? For one thing, demand for the art fell at the turn of the century, when fancy Victorian aesthetics gave way in a push for streamlined modernization. Such a relatively short spell of disfavor should hardly have effected the longevity of an age-old

craft, though, had it not been for craftsmen who shared their "secrets" only with apprentices and sons, and reclusive monks who died without leaving heirs to the art. Even today, the few craftsmen who've inherited the formulas and techniques for genuine gold leafing guard them like state secrets. Unfortunately, good craftsmen often maintain their status in the field by being the only ones in the field. Some go so far as to give out incorrect and incomplete formulas in order to keep others from attaining success in their exclusive field.

Relatively few proficient gilders can be found today, and their costly services are absorbed by art galleries and manufacturers of expensive new frames and furniture. Even in large metropolitan cities, few art dealers or frame shops can provide gold leafing services for their customers.

Yet there's a great demand for the art as people seek to save and restore antiques left from a more gilded age. Plus there are more heirlooms to be made, with gold leaf improving everything from frames, wood carvings, furniture, and architectural moldings to household items like lamps and clocks.

Despite the mystique, gilding is not nearly as difficult as it may seem. With patience and practice, almost anyone can learn to apply and burnish gold leaf. This book explains basic techniques and walks beginners through a series of projects, from basic restoration techniques, to working with the relatively easy-to-handle Dutch metal, to water and oil gilding techniques with 23-karat gold. It is recommended that you read this book through from beginning to end, then pick a project related to those illustrated in the book. Start with something simple, like the Dutch metal project, and work your way up to more complicated undertakings.

Good luck to you in your artistic endeavors. Remember—you are not only giving a new lease to old treasures and creating treasures for the future. You are also keeping alive a craft indelibly linked with human kind's highest artistic accomplishments.

# Chapter 1

# TOOLS AND SUPPLIES

## Types of Brushes

Camel hair quill brush, #12: For touching leaf into place.

Camel hair wash, #1: Used for dusting.

Flat bristle brush: 1/4 inch, 1/2 inch, 3/4 inch: For thick coating.

Flat sable, #2, #8, #12, #16: The most frequently used brushes in gilding.

Gilder's tip.

Large round sable brush, #12: For applying alcohol/water mixture for water gilding.

Round sable brush, #2, #0: For spotting and antiquing.

Stencil brush, #7: For cleaning carving and hollows.

## Getting Started

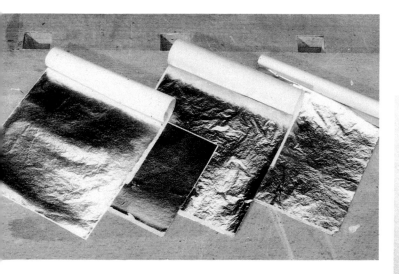

I keep assorted brushes and carving tools handy in my work studio. For a list of brushes, see boxed item above.

Though a variety of tools are useful for carving and shaping compo ornaments, I use any kind of tool that works. Every artist has their favorites.

Besides 23-karat German gold leaf, other metals that can be used for leafing include silver, bronze, Dutch metal, and copper leaf.

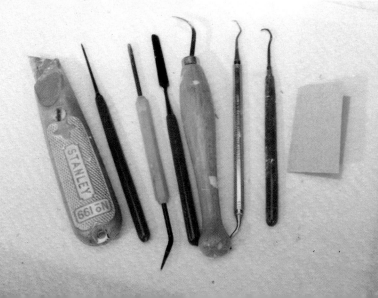

After applying varnish, I clean my brushes with turpentine and then rinse them with L.O.C., a product made by Amway. After using shellac, I use isopropyl alcohol and then rinse them in L.O.C. Allow brushes to soak in L.O.C. overnight, then rinse them with water.

Burnishing tools.

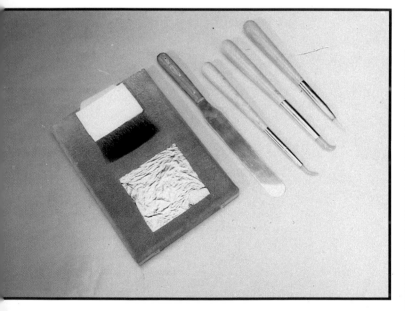

Gilder's tip of squirrel and camel hair, used to pick up gold; 23K German gold leaf; 6 x 10 inch gilder's cushion; gilder's knife for cutting gold and other metals; and three different-sizes of burnishing stones, which are only used for water gilding.

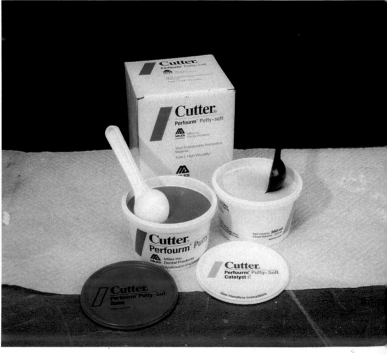

This is dental impression made by Cutter, used to make molds in restoration work.

I prefer to use the milk-based Casein colors for antiquing. These are two of my favorites, though they come in many colors, for antiquing any of the metals and gold.

This is orange shellac—a mixture of two parts alcohol, one part orange shellac crystals, soaked overnight and stirred frequently until dissolved. It should be used over any kind of metal to seal it and prevent any tarnishing. You don't have to use shellac with gold, which doesn't tarnish.

This photo shows rabbit skin glue that has been melted down in a jar behind a sheet of rabbit skin glue; as well as bole clay in red and yellow, soaking in water; and a cone of dry red bole.

# Making Rabbit Skin Glue

Weigh out 100 grams of dried rabbit skin glue.

Stir to wet thoroughly and allow to stand overnight or until it expands.

Mix 100 grams of rabbit skin glue mix with 3-1/4 cups of water and soak overnight.

The rabbit skin glue will swell up. The following day, melt mixture in a double broiler until smooth. Store in a refrigerator.

# Making Bole

Bole should be liquefied to the point where it will drip off the brush.

Dry clay needs to soak in water for about one hour to soften. Here yellow bole is ready to mix with rabbit skin glue in a 50/50 mix.

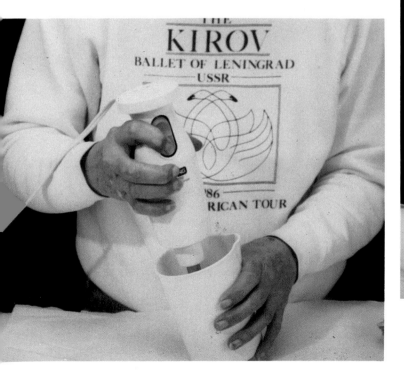

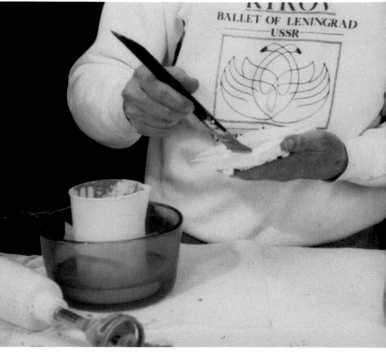

Keep bole in a pot of warm water to keep it warm while you work.

Mix bole and rabbit skin glue with a hand mixer until smooth.

Repeat the same mixing process with red bole and an equal amount of rabbit skin glue. When you are done working with it, put it in the refrigerator immediately to extend its shelf life. Keep it refrigerated.

## Making Compo

## Making Gesso

4 parts 50/50 rabbit skin glue/water
2 parts water
8 parts whiting

Rabbit skin glue should be pre-made at least a day before and ready to go. Heat in double broiler and then mix add water. Keep the double broiler on low heat and work it and stir it. Stir in whiting, adding gradually and stirring very slowly until it eventually forms a skin on top. Remove this skin as it will have a lot of air bubbles. You do not want any air bubbles in your gesso. If I am not sure it is smooth enough, I put it through a strainer.

Keep gesso refrigerated. Take out small portions to work withand heat them in a double broiler. As you are brushing the gesso onto a frame or any object you are working on, you want to keep it warm—only warm. Do not overheat or it will break down the strength of the glue. Brush it on as smoothly as you possibly can. The smoother you get it on, the more time you save yourself in hand sanding.

Prepare by placing a dozen or more squares of plastic wrap nearby to be wrap compo patties later.

You will need a tin can and a burner.

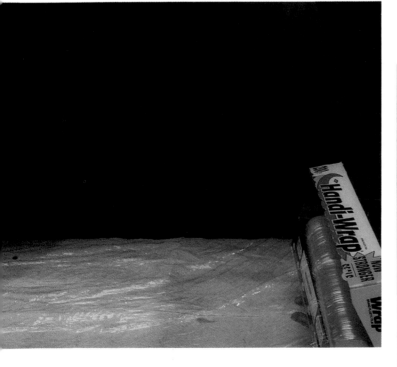

Spread plastic wrap on work surface.

Add three tablespoons of linseed oil to can and heat on low.

Add resin chunks. Melt that in the linseed oil. Stir often.

Mix resin mixture with warm glue.

Heat rabbit-skin glue mixture in a double broiler until liquefied and slightly warm.

Put a cup and three quarters of 50/50 rabbit-skin glue and pearl hide glue in double broiler.

Use four parts glue mixture and two parts warm water.

Add eight parts sifted whiting, adding gradually while mixing into rabbit-skin/water mixture.

Add whiting until it gets thick enough, about the consistency of a bread dough (about a cup and one third).

Mix well.

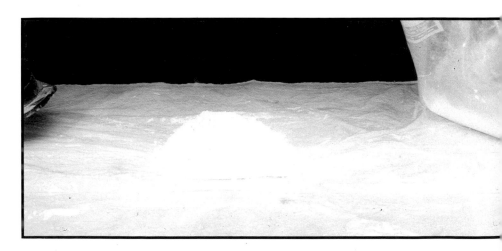

Put about a cup of whiting on the plastic-covered work surface.

Pour about a half cup of the heated mixture into a hole in the whiting.

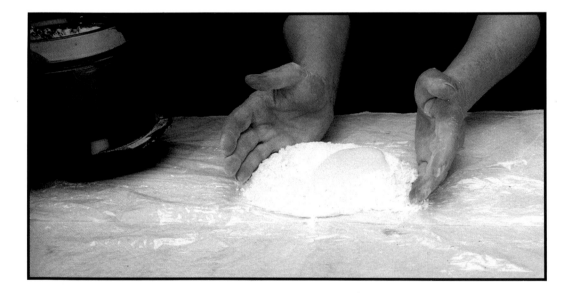

Pick up mixture and knead.

Work it until it becomes very solid. It should be very pliable

If it becomes too dry, add a little water.

Put into a plastic container, cover, and refrigerate until ready to use.

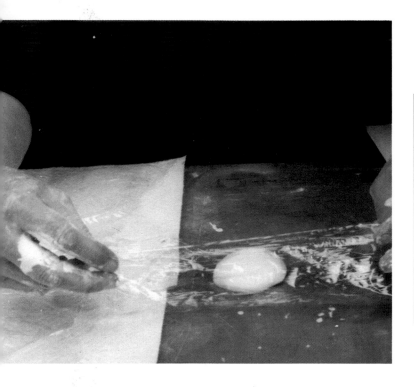

Wrap patty in a square of plastic wrap.

# Making Orange Shellac

2 parts 99% isopropyl alcohol
1 part orange shellac crystals

Put into a jar and stir frequently. It takes approximately two days to completely dissolve. It will feel really sticky on the bottom of the jar. Keep working it and it will develop into a nice smooth liquid that will create a beautiful finish.

# CHAPTER 2

# RESTORATION TECHNIQUES

Before and after pictures of a frame partially restored and gilded in this book. The broken pineapple ornament is repaired later in this chapter. In the before photos, the outer white square has already been gessoed. It is gold leafed in Chapter Six.

Before

Another frame restored in this chapter. The broken outer ornaments are repaired and replaced, with all the pieces that can be saved salvaged. A mold is cast of the upper portion of the frame to create a new strip of ornamentation for the badly damaged bottom of the frame.

# Cleaning and Stripping

This is a roll of cotton used in leg wrappings for horses. It is sold in feed stores for about $6 a roll. The blue Kutzit® is a stripper sold in hardware stores. The plastic storage unit with the hole in the top is a useful waste receptacle.

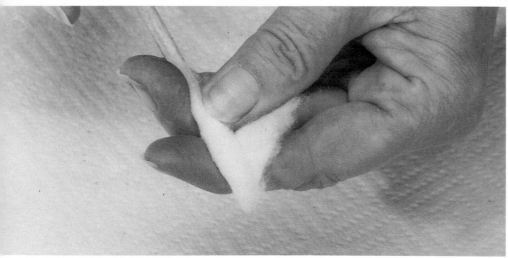

Take a small piece of cotton and roll onto stick to create a tool for cleaning.

To minimize fumes, dip cotton into jar of Kutzit® and cover with lid as soon as possible.

Apply Kutzit® to area to be stripped down to the silver-leaf. Allow it to sit for a minute.

Use the same tool to rewipe the area and remove dirt.

Remove dirty cotton from stick. A small hole in a lidded container is another way to help minimize fumes and odor.

Using a fresh piece of cotton dipped in alcohol to remove dirt and remaining Kutzit®. Follow this with L.O.C., an organic detergent from Amway. You may need to repeat the preceding process several times.

Compare cleaned and dirty portions. At this point I realized I was not able to salvage what was underneath the silver. I decided I was going to have to hand-sand and remove all the old gesso.

Remove the silver with 100-grit sandpaper.

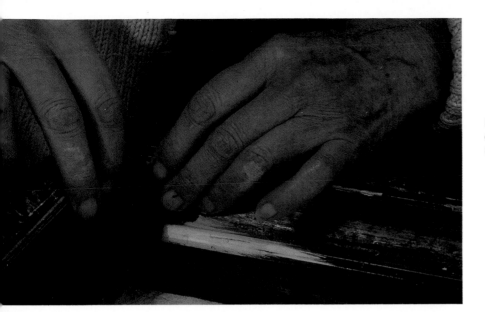

Place cloth soaked in warm water over old gesso to soften it for several minutes.

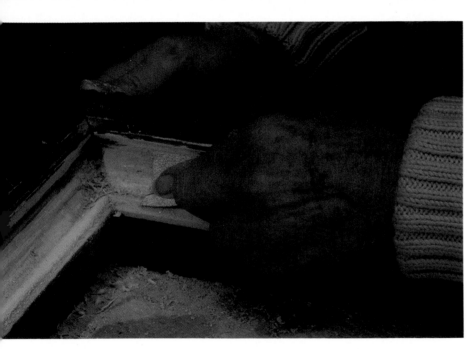

Remove dampened gesso with 100-grit sandpaper. All of the gesso will have to go.

You can also use metal tools to scrape off thicker layers of gesso.

The wet rag can soak one portion of the frame while you scrape another.

Use large brush to remove dust. Keeping a small vacuum handy to help reduce dust in the work environment.

From this angle you can see how the silver leaf lining has been sanded away on the newly re-molded side, paired with the untouched frame liner.

# Repairing a Joint

Use a razor or knife to remove any old pieces of gesso or debris from the corner seam before sealing.

Put wood filler in the crack and allow it to dry.

Put white glue or five-minute epoxy in the corner.

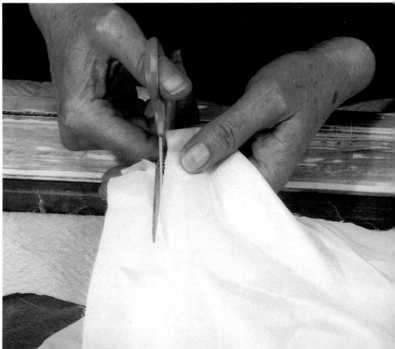

Cut a 1-inch strip of silk to fill corners.

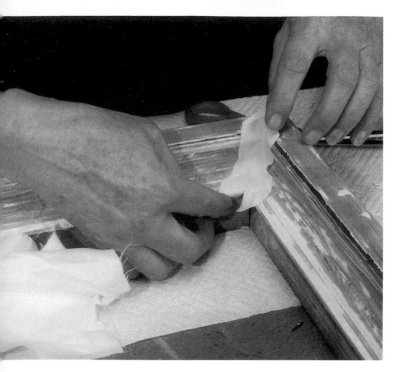

Play with silk strip and cut it to fit corner.

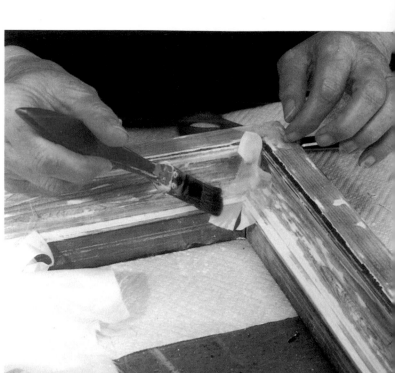

Set silk in the corner and apply more rabbit-skin glue as needed to hold it in place. Let it dry overnight.

Apply warm rabbit-skin glue in corner.

Trim away excess silk. It's important to get the silk to lay flat. Now you can begin with gesso.

# Replacing Lost or Broken Ornaments

The ornamentation on this frame was destroyed by severe temperatures—too hot or too cold. Unfortunately, many antique frames end up in attics and basements.

You can reattach broken ornaments. Use white glue or five-minute epoxy on all frame and ornament surfaces that will touch, then press firmly into place. Allow to dry before attempting to replace adjacent pieces.

Another broken spot on the frame is prepared for patching, with all excess gesso sanded away.

These two pieces will now fill the empty space left by a broken ornament. Once gessoed and leafed, the inconsistencies in pattern will be discernible only to the most critical eyes.

Here the back of a salvaged ornament is coated with five-minute epoxy.

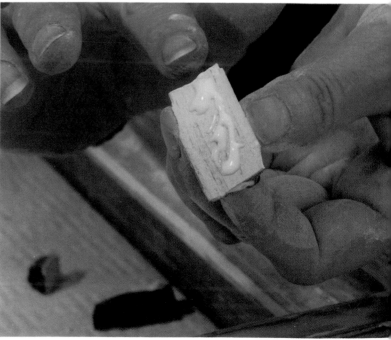

The pieces are sanded down to fit in the hole.

Don't forget to apply glue to the sides that will butt up against other ornaments on the frame.

Place the piece firmly on the frame and hold or clamp until the ornament is secure.

On the other hand, this crack between repaired ornaments is too obvious. We will fill it with gesso.

It is not necessary to repair a crack like this. It's part of the antique look and part of the charm of the frame.

Put rabbit skin glue in the crack.

Then fill it with gesso. You must let the gesso dry before adding new layers. This will take up to twelve more applications to fill the crack.

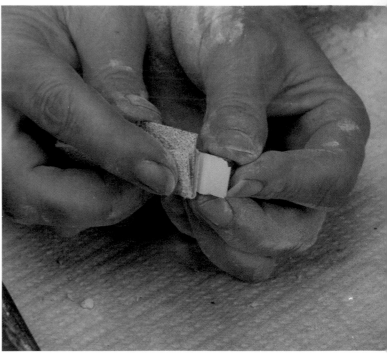

A broken ornament is sanded to fit.

These five loose ornaments will be used to complete a stretch of bare frame.

Apply white glue or five-minute epoxy to the frame.

Spread glue evenly over surface to be patched and on ornaments, then attach.

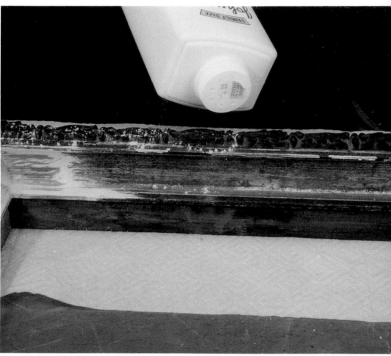

Apply talcum powder to the ornamentation.

To patch larger sections of missing ornaments, we first find a good section of frame to make an impression of, like that on the far side of the frame.

Brush powder in lightly to smooth it out.

Mix about three scoops of blue dental impression, three of white.

Press the dental impression over the mold, firmly pressing to fill all the cracks.

Knead quickly to thoroughly mix. After you mix the two you have about five minutes to apply the dental impression over the ornaments before it dries.

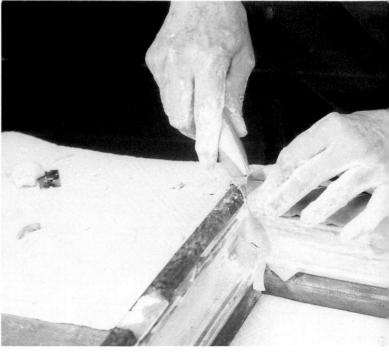

Trim excess dental impression from the corners and allow it to dry for about 20 minutes.

Loosen edges of dental impression and remove gently.

Remove loose ornaments from the frame.

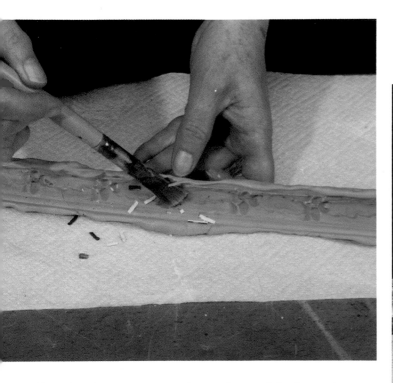

Use a brush to remove any loose pieces of the frame that pulled off in the mold.

The gesso is removed from one side of the frame, along with loose ornaments.

Seal wood with warm rabbit kin glue.

Apply white glue or five-minute epoxy and spread evenly over the surface to be molded.

Apply a small piece of compo to the surface to be molded.

34

Continue the process for the entire area to be patched.

To join rolls of compo, the seal the seam with a little water.

Trim off any overhang and even out the compo.

Sprinkle a little bit of talcum powder into the mold.

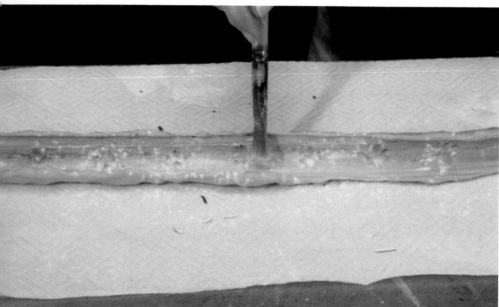
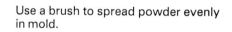

Use a brush to spread powder evenly in mold.

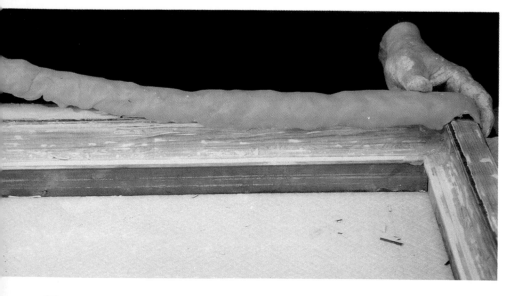

Place the mold over the compo and press down carefully.

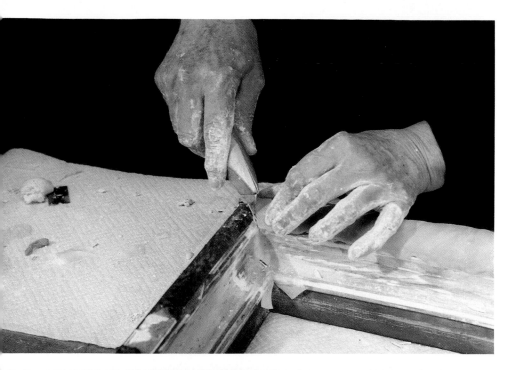

Trim the corner, if needed, to fit snugly against existing ornaments.

Allow to sit for about ten minutes, then carefully remove.

This area of the mold is too wide and we need to trim and shape it a little bit more.

Use sandpaper to work down raised areas and improve the design. This process is much easier when the compo is still damp, fresh out of the mold. Then you can use a knife to shape and trim it.

Use carving tools to help shape the newly molded ornaments. Be careful, however, that you don't cut too deep or you can crack the ornament.

Use sandpaper to smooth and bring out details in the molding, helping to define and sculpt it. You may also use a small hobby drill.

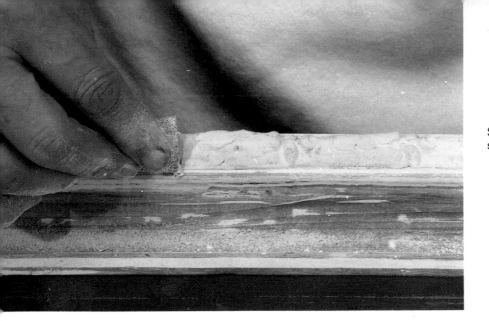

Smooth the edges with 150-grit sandpaper.

Here a corner shows the new mold next to the original frame.

## Making a Mold for Patching

This pineapple ornament was badly cracked. This and other pieces of the frame were stabilized immediately with pieces of wood glued on with five-minute epoxy.

The patch on the pineapple ornament, from the back.

Prepare the surface of the ornament to be repaired by sanding away previous gold leaf and gesso.

A knife or other gilding tools can be used to gently pry away old gesso.

A knife can be used to gently scrape away old gesso, but be careful not to cut into the original wood carving.

Here we are sanding down a good pineapple ornament in order to make a duplicate for the other side of the frame. To make a mold, we must remove the old gesso and partial gilding.

It is important to reveal as much of the bare wood as possible.

Powder the ornament lightly.

Mix equal parts of blue and white dental mold.

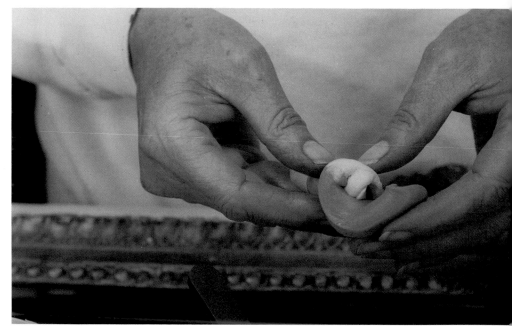

Press dental mold over sanded ornament. Allow to harden.

Carefully pry dental mold loose and remove.

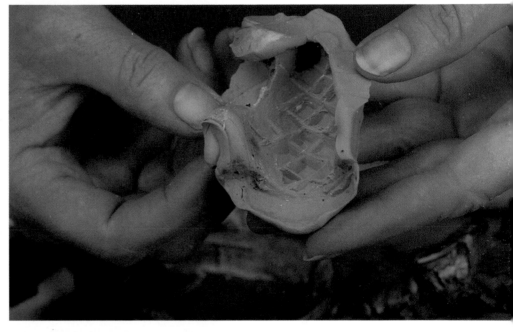

This is a nice one, with the grooves showing nice and clear.

Try the mold out in the intended location. Here a piece on top is too big and will need to be removed.

Without the protruding piece cut away, this mold will be easier to place.

Cut all of the excess off.

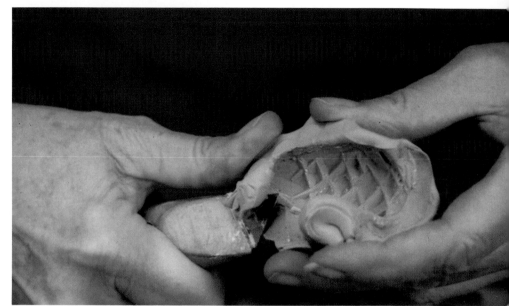

The trimmed mold...

... fits easily into place now.

Brush away any remaining dust. The ornament is ready for a compo mold.

Apply white glue. Spread evenly over the surface to be ornamented.

Press compo into place, thoroughly covering the patch area.

Immediately remove the patch and shape it.

Press the mold down over the compo.

After the mold has dried, you can further refine it by carving and sanding. Here I remove dust with a brush.

# CHAPTER 3
# Basic Techniques for Gilding

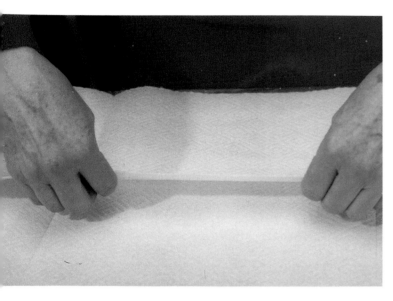

A clean surface is crucial in gold leafing.

I wipe the gilder's knife with a paper towel to clean it...

... and then with my hands so that I get some oil on the side of it. In the winter time, it's good to have humidity in the air where you are working. A pot of boiling water will put humidity into the air and reduce static.

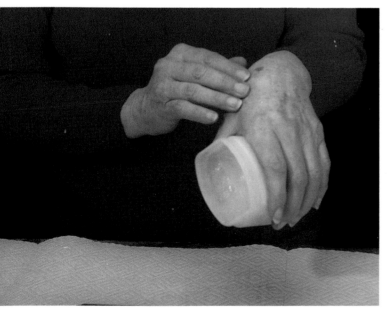

Apply petroleum jelly to hands.

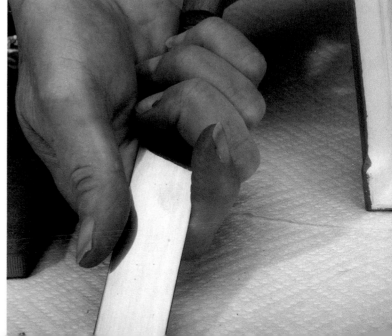

Any dirt or remaining gold on the knife, as well as static, will cause a jagged cut.

Without touching the metal, put two sheets of gold on the gilder's pad...

Make sure that the gilder's pad is clean before applying new sheets of gold.

...Like so. I only use 23-karat German gold leaf.

Cut the gold sheets with the gilder's knife...

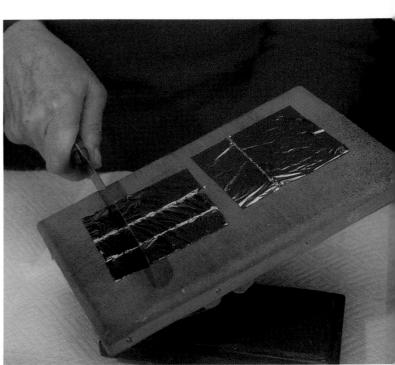

The size of the pieces depends on the subject.

...like so.

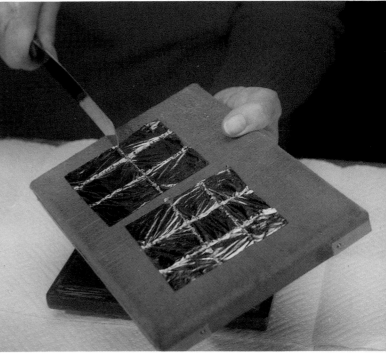

I've given myself various sizes to work with here.

Get petroleum jelly from your arm onto the gilder's tip.

Between applications, remove scraps of gold leaf by running the tip along the edge of a collection box so that nothing is wasted. Keep different collection boxes for scraps of all the metals you use, that way nothing is wasted.

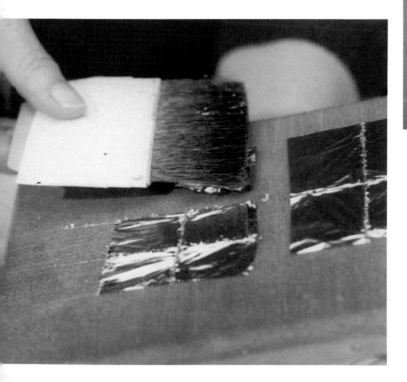

Use the gilder's tip to pick up a piece of gold.

# CHAPTER 4
# DUTCH METAL PROJECT

This is a project simple enough for any age or experience level.

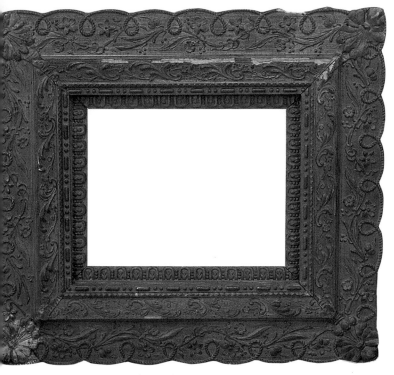

A frame before refinishing.

The same frame after Dutch metal leafing and antiquing.

Brush off any dirt and dust from the surface to be gilded and then clean with L.O.C., a product from Amway, to prepare the surface to be gilded. Before gilding with Dutch metal, hand paint the frame with an oil-base paint. A maroon color works well.

Very gently remove the frame liner.

Apply Quick-dry Synthetic Gold Size to the area to be gilded.

Use short, quick strokes to coat evenly. Use small amounts and spread thinly. Allow to dry for one to three hours.

Use your knuckle to check the lacquer. When it feels just slightly tacky, then you are ready to apply Dutch metal.

Lay a sheet of Dutch metal on the gilder's pad.

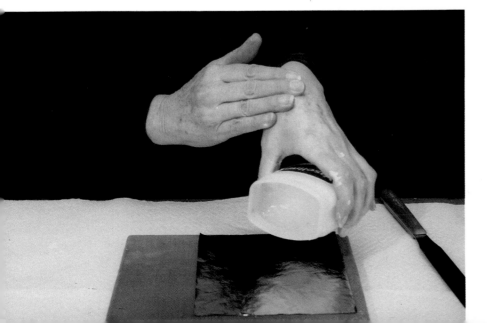

Apply a little Vaseline on your hand to prevent static when picking up and working with the Dutch metal.

Also, apply a very thin film of petroleum jelly to the gilder's knife to prevent static. Talcum powder is another great way to reduce static.

Cut Dutch metal into strips approximately one-inch wide.

Then cut the Dutch metal into squares.

Place the squares on the frame and dab down with a flat brush.

Use small squares and press them on. With Dutch metal you can use a thumb or finger to patch missed spots. If the Gold Size dries on you, you can go back over it after applying all the Dutch metal. Apply Gold Size to bare spots and again wait for it to dry to a slightly tacky consistency.

Brush powdered brass over bare surfaces to reach small crevices and create an even, smooth surface.

Use powdered brass and a brush to remove loose flakes. Capture these in a box or on a paper towel and save them for future use.

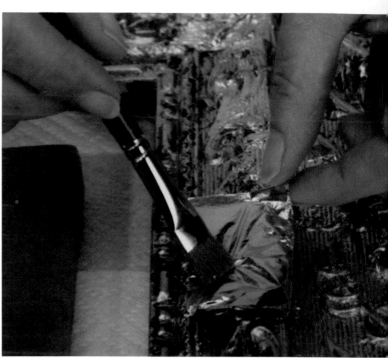

After the Gold Size has dried to a tacky consistency, use small squares of Dutch metal to patch, again patting them into place with a dry brush.

To patch places where the Gold Size dried unevenly and Dutch metal didn't stick, reapply Gold Size and allow to dry until tacky.

Repeat this process on the frame liner. For parts with deep crevices, a second sheet on top of the first may be required.

# CHAPTER 5
# ANTIQUING

Start with a dab of raw umber and a dab of yellow ochre, for antiquing, along with a dish and a little water for mixing.

Wet a brush and mix a small amount of each color, swirling without blending completely.

Dip sponge into paint mix, don't smear.

Dab paint on frame lightly.

A brush can be used to get a more thorough coat of antiquing paint.

Use the brush to apply paint to areas to be darkened such as the loops in the faux rope here.

... and detailing along the inner border,...

... and background areas.

Press a paper towel to the surface to remove excess paint. Remember, paint will dry lighter.

Use a piece of clean linen to remove any paint from the parts I want to be shiny. At this point you should examine the frame from a distance and under different lighting to judge the effect.

Try to even out antique paint and allow it to dry.

Remove excess paint from the raised surfaces of ornaments, allowing the background to remain dark.

Use a piece of linen to wipe down the frame after the antiquing paint has dried.

60

This polishes the frame. Now we will go in with more antiquing to try to even out areas and create more contrast.

Apply a light, thin coat of shellac.

Now it looks much better. With antiquing you don't want it too even.

The shellac will seal the Dutch metal and prevent it from tarnishing. The shellac can be removed with alcohol.

# CHAPTER 6

# Water Gilding

Layers of gesso have been applied around the outer frame. I am sanding here to see whether the gesso is high enough to even it out with the rest of the frame.

This small chip broke away from the frame during the sanding process. We will replace it and do additional repairs to this corner.

Use folded sandpaper to get definition.

First fill the crevice with white glue or five-minute epoxy.

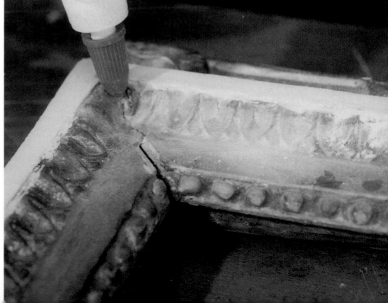

Carefully fit the broken piece back into place.

Work white glue into the crack.

With the broken piece replaced, the corner still needs a little patching.

Then work wood putty into the crack using small tools.

Use your finger to smooth the patch.

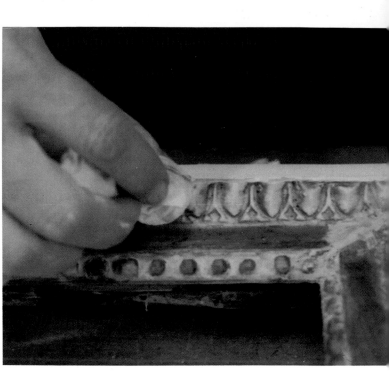

Use a lightly dampened cloth to remove dust from sanding.

The finished wood putty patch should be left to dry for about two hours.

Apply yellow bole in short even strokes.

I like to put it on thin. If it's thick it shows too many brush strokes. I would rather add an extra coat.

For water gilding, you want a good thickness to the bole, so I will do four coats of yellow bole. Try to apply them as evenly as possible.

A hairdryer can help speed the drying process between coats of bole. The bole may help point out flaws in the sanding job. It is not too late to get out your gilder's tools or sandpaper and correct any errors before continuing with the bole application.

After the four coats of yellow bole, we add four coats of red.

If you get too much bole in a crevice, you can gently hand sand it with extra fine, 320-grit sandpaper.

Buff with a piece of dry linen.

After the eight layers of bole dry, polish them. Start with a slightly damp piece of linen and dampen the bole.

To begin gilding, we need to have gilding tools, gold, water, and 99 percent isopropyl alcohol at hand.

Mix seven parts water with three parts 99% isopropyl alcohol.

Brush alcohol/water mixture on a small area of the surface to be gilded.

Prop up one corner of the frame about 1/4 to 1/2 inch so that the water/alcohol solution will run, but not into the areas of the frame that won't be gilded.

Apply gold to wet areas.

Use a dry brush to pat pieces of gold into place.

After it is applied, the gold should sit for about three hours.

If there are any areas where the gold did not adhere, first apply a little alcohol/water mixture and re-gild.

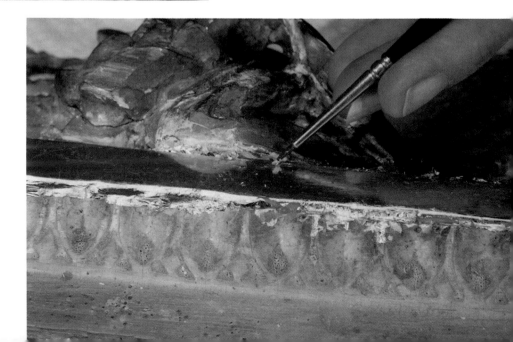

A dry brush can be used to pick up small pieces of gold for patching.

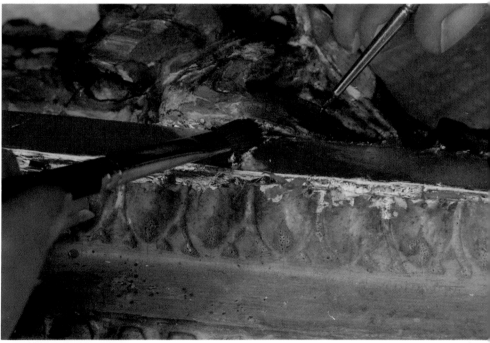

Place the small patch on the dampened section of frame with the dry brush.

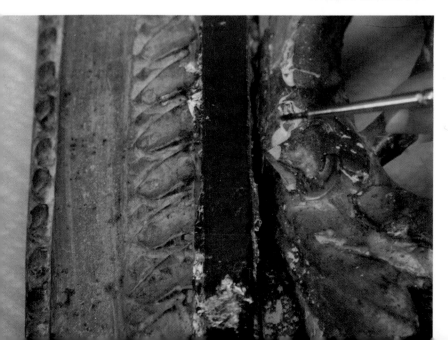

Another patch—water first...

... followed by gold leaf. Allow the patches to dry for approximately three hours before burnishing.

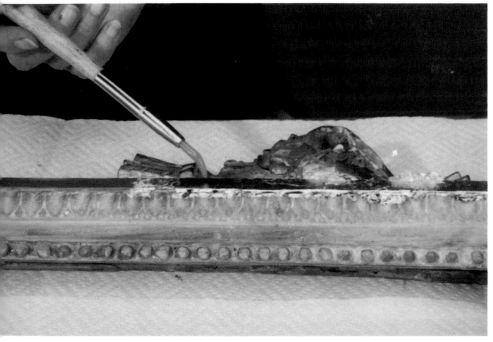

In order to find out if you are ready to do the burnishing, tap with a burnishing tool on the gold...

... and on the dried and buffed bole. They should sound the same. If they don't, the work needs to sit and dry some more, at least one hour longer depending on humidity.

This work is ready. Polish by working in a circular motion in very small sections. Here I am working with a size 21 burnishing stone.

This works out all the roughness and polishes the gold.

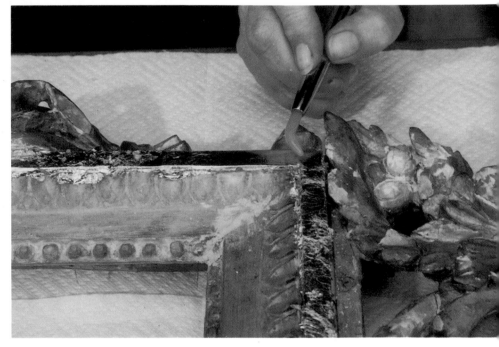

Apply a little pressure. Sometimes some of the clay will show through, and that's all right. That's why you put the different colors of bole down in the first place—so you can see the different colors coming through. This will give the water gilding a very high, polished look. If you like, you may antique it.

# CHAPTER 7

# BOX PROJECTS

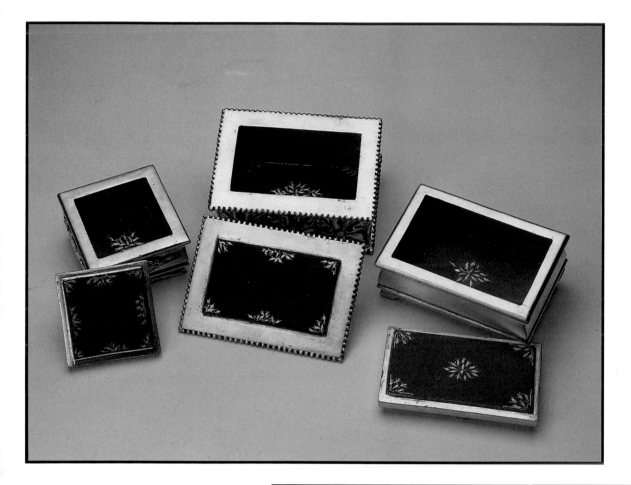

These box and funeral urn projects are possible using the following techniques.

# Applying Ornaments

These ornaments were purchased from The Decorator Supply Corp. in Chicago. They are pictured as bought, with bole applied, and oil gilded.

Inside of the Alexandria box.

This is the Alexandria box. To start, the raw wood was hand sanded and sealed with rabbit-skin glue. The ornaments were steamed and glued on. Then several of what will total about fourteen coats of gesso were applied by brush.

The Victoria box with ornament and several coats of gesso.

Inside of the Victoria box.

## Applying Gesso

Compare the smaller lid, which looks shinier and darker because its last coat of gesso is still wet, with the longer lid that is ready for a second coat of gesso.

Apply a thin coat of gesso. Allow to dry for a couple of minutes until it looks dull, then apply the next coat.

Because you need 14 coats of gesso, you may want to carry the task out over several days. Whenever you stop gesso work, allow it to dry, and resume adding coats later, you need to first seal it with a half-and-half rabbit-skin glue/water mixture.

After twelve to fourteen coats, allow to dry overnight.

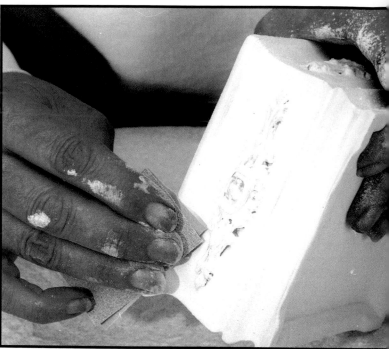

Remove major bumps and smooth with 150-grit sandpaper. Follow-up with 220- to 320-grit until the piece feels super smooth.

Hand sand the gesso, making it very smooth.

Hand sand the ornaments and surrounding areas.

After sanding with 220- to 320-grit sandpaper, remove any remaining dust with a damp paper towel.

## Applying Bole

Apply it carefully on the inside.

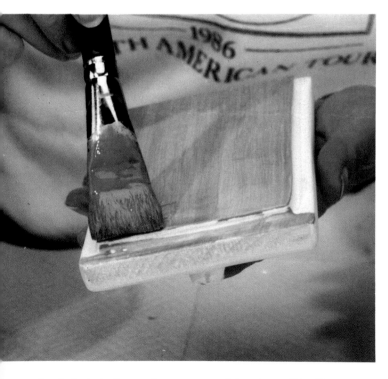

Apply bole to the surface as smoothly as possible. The smoother you get it on, the less sanding you have to do later.

In applying the bole to an ornament, make sure to fill in all the crevices, then go over it with the brush to smooth it out.

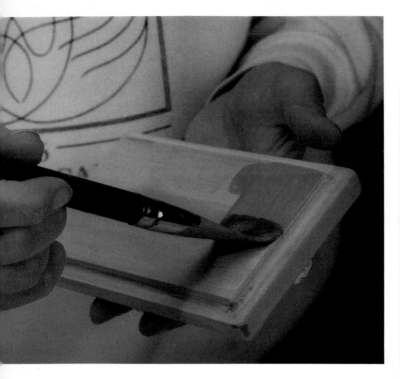

Allow the bole to dry about ten minutes—it will look lighter in color—before applying a second coat. Follow-up with a third coat after the second has dried.

Apply three coats of red or black bole over yellow in the same manner.

A small hair dryer can help speed the drying process between coats of bole. Use a cool setting, however. Extreme temperatures will cause the clay to crack.

After four coats of yellow bole and four coats of red bole, the pieces should set and dry completely for 24 hours. Then the boxes are ready for buffing or light sanding.

Slightly dampen a small piece of linen.

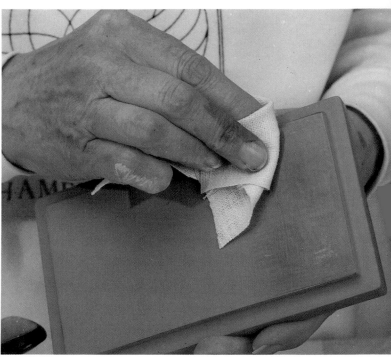

Use a dry piece of linen and buff to a shine. This is especially good for water gilding.

Dampen a small area of the surface to be buffed.

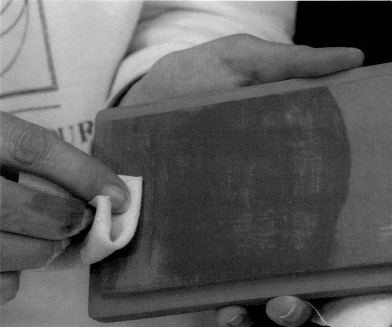

It is okay if yellow bole shines through. This will lend different highlights to the gold.

Use cloth folded up to reach into cracks.

Make sure that your damp cloth isn't too wet and that you don't add too much water, even though the clay will absorb some. Your dry cloth should remain dry.

Feel the surface to make sure it's smooth and that there aren't any little bubbles in it.

Follow the same procedure for polishing the bole on the ornaments.

# Oil Gilding the Inside of a Box

A patch is placed in the corner. Every job is different, with its own strange angles to overcome.

When gilding the inside of an object, it is best just to do the bottom and two sides. Gold Size has been added to the bottom and to sides so that two sides remain dry. It will take a little longer, but save a lot of aggravation.

A dry, clean brush can help to spread loose flakes and patch holes.

Applying the gold inside the box.

A little touch up work on the inside of the box before moving on to the final two inside sides.

After gold leafing the bottom and two sides, add Gold Size to the other two sides and allow to set until it obtains the right degree of tackiness.

Leaf the other two inside sides.

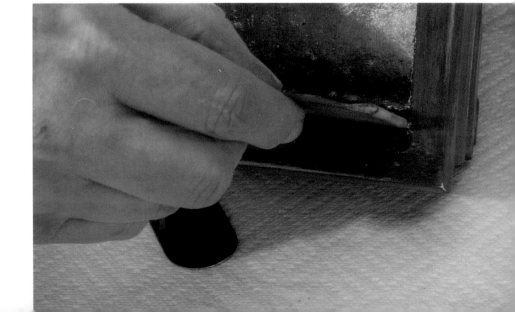

# Oil Gilding the Outside of a Box

I am going to water gild the top portion of this box, and oil gild the lower portion.

The box is propped up on its side to make sure that the water/alcohol mixture drains evenly.

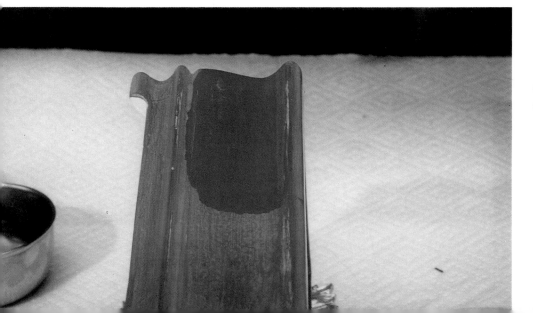

Water alcohol mixture is applied to a small section.

Gold leaf is placed on the wet surface.

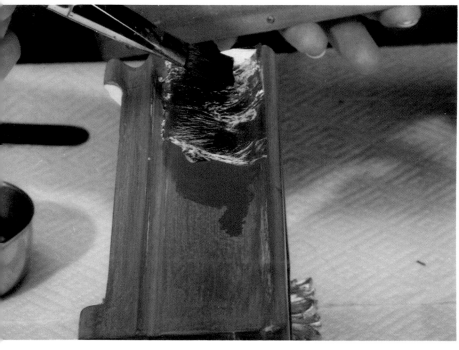

Use a brush wet in the alcohol/water mixture for any touch-up work, then apply more leaf on top.

Wrinkles like these are no big deal—they will burnish out.

This small, missed spot at the corner of the gilder's tip can easily be touched up.

Wet the spot to be patched with alcohol/water mixture and then apply a small piece of gold.

Finished, the gold must be left to set for about three hours, more if it's humid, less if it's dry. It is important not to touch the gold with your fingers until after it has been burnished.

When the gold has set, tap it with your gilding tool and tap an area of bole. If they sound the same, you are ready to burnish to smooth and polish the gold leaf.

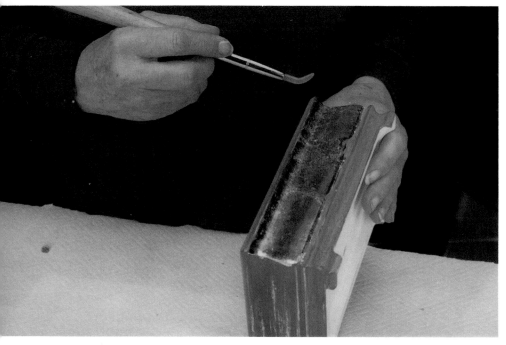

After the burnishing is done, the gold can be handled. It can be antiqued now, too, if you like.

Apply Gold Size to areas of box to be oil gilded.

Gold leaf is applied to the top and bottom sections of the long box.

Like so.

See the more matte finish of oil gilding versus water gilding.

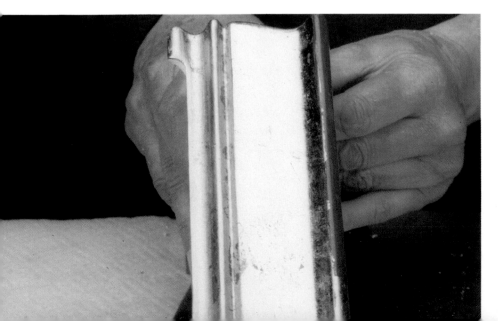

# Gilding the Lid

Using long, even strokes, apply a thin coat of Gold Size. It is best to do the inside first because when it is done you don't have to handle it as much.

When the Gold Size has dried to a tacky consistency, begin to apply the gold.

Continue the process until the surface is covered.

All excess gold should be brushed into a box.

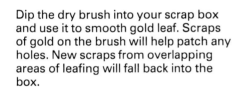

Dip the dry brush into your scrap box and use it to smooth gold leaf. Scraps of gold on the brush will help patch any holes. New scraps from overlapping areas of leafing will fall back into the box.

Some patching will be necessary in the corners.

# Gilding the Ornament

Apply a thin layer of Gold Size to ornament. To prevent excess in cracks and crevasses, don't overload your brush.

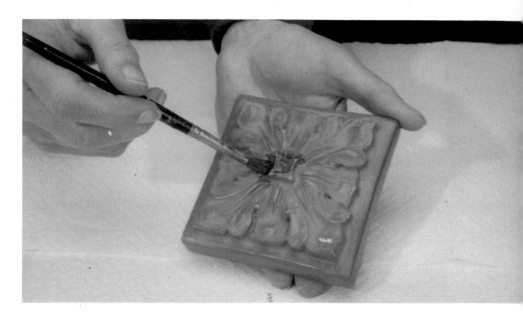

When the Gold Size has dried to a tacky consistency, you can gold leaf the ornament.

Don't worry if leaf is wrinkly. A brush will straighten that right out.

Use gold flakes and a dry brush to help reach any missed crevices and smooth the work.

# Painting Over Gold Leaf

We will now paint the inside of the box lid using high-quality latex paint.

Give it an even, generous coat. If one coat covers, that's all you need. Sometimes two coats are necessary.

Do the same for the bottom of the inside of the box.

Use a really good artists brush rather than a paint brush to help minimize brush strokes.

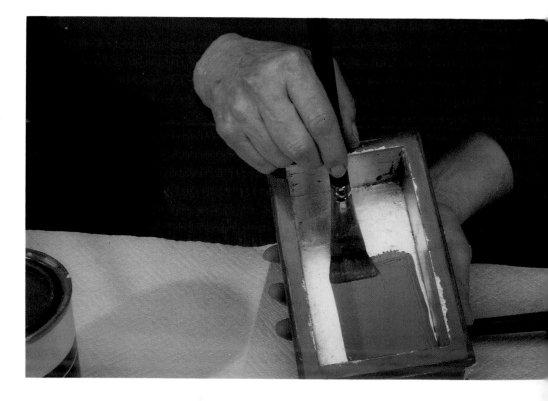

After the paint dries, use a sharp metal tool to etch a line.

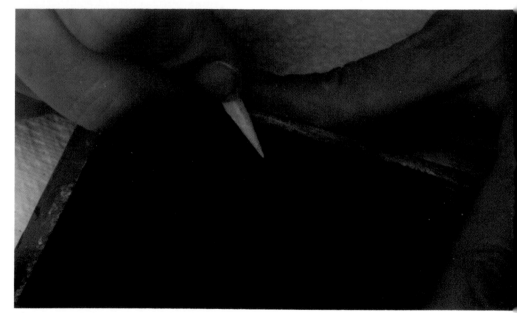

Use a sharp wooden stick to lightly scrape away larger sections of paint to expose the gold.

Use a dry brush to remove flakes of paint. Antique and seal the painted area with low-luster clear varnish. I use McCloskey Heirloom Clear Varnish.

93

# Resource List

The Decorators Supply Corp.
Chicago, Illinois
777-847-6357

W & B Gold Leaf
Chicago, Illinois
773-472-1544

BAGGOT LEAF COMPANY
430 BROOME STREET
NEW YORK, NY 10013-3260
(212)431-GOLD or FAX: (212)431-3962

# Other Titles from Schiffer Publishing

**The Art of Marquetry** Craig Vandall Stevens. *Text written with and photography by Joy Shih Ng.* Marquetry is a technique where different natural colors of wood veneers are carefully fit precisely together, creating a spectacular design. Using the double-bevel cut, the woodworker is led through a fully illustrated step-by-step process from the design to the finish. Hundreds of color photographs demonstrate the technique. Four patterns ranging from simple to challenging projects are included as is an extended gallery of finished works to inspire the marquetarian in you.

| | | |
|---|---|---|
| Size: 8 1/2" x 11" | 400 color photos, instructions | 96 pp. |
| ISBN: 0-7643-0237-X | soft cover | $16.95 |

**Finishes for Wood** Dale Power. *Text written with, and photography by, Jeffrey B. Snyder.* A step-by-step finishing school, featuring fourteen different techniques for refining wood surfaces. All of the tools and methods needed to successfully change the image of any wooden surface are covered. More than 200 color photographs accompany the text. In addition, there are instructions for restoring damaged finishes, and a color gallery provides a final look at all of the finishes.

| | | |
|---|---|---|
| Size: 8 1/2" x 11" | 200 color photos | 64pp. |
| ISBN: 0-7643-0338-4 | soft cover | $14.95 |

**Authentic Antique Stenciling** Gen Ventrone. The charm of stenciled decorations has appealed to people for hundreds of years. Shown here are many old examples of stenciling on tin, furniture, glass, velvet, and walls. Using patterns of designs taken from old stencils, there are step-by-step instructions for their reproduction, with color photographs and a full explanatory text.

| | | |
|---|---|---|
| Size: 8 1/2" x 11" | b/w and color photos/drawings | 176 pp. |
| Index | | |
| ISBN: 0-88740-140-6 | soft cover | $19.95 |

**Stenciling: 140 Historical Patterns for Room Decoration** Ilse Maierbacher. Room stenciling is more popular today than ever before. This book illustrates 140 historic ornaments spanning the past century. Examples of colorfully decorated spaces provide additional inspiration, with floral and geometric, light and bright motifs. Detailed directions for simple as well as complex designs make the easily learned techniques a pleasure to use. With little expense necessary for tools and materials, this is a reasonably priced hobby that you can discover anew here!

| | | |
|---|---|---|
| Size: 8 1/2" x 11" | 191 photos/140 stencil patterns | 128 pp. |
| ISBN: 0-7643-0376-7 | soft cover | $24.95 |

**Reupholstering at Home** Peter Nesovich. Step-by-step instructions with 350 clear and detailed photographs show how to rebuild that dilapidated chair or sofa to look like new. Covered are the tools and materials you will need, and expert advice about which types of fabric are best for your needs. The author offers specific steps through text, photographs, and captions.

| | | |
|---|---|---|
| Size:81/2" x 11" | 350 Photos | 176 pp. |
| ISBN:0-88740-376-X | soft cover | $14.95 |

**Making Classic Carved Furniture: The Queen Anne Stool** Ron Clarkson & Tom Heller. *Text written with and photography by Douglas Congdon-Martin.* Step by step through the process of making a beautiful carved Queen Anne foot stool. Complete instructions are given, with an emphasis on the classic carving that added such elegance to period furniture. You will learn which carving tools to use and how to apply them to this project. Complete measured drawings are supplied with the full-sized detailed drawings. Each step,from cutting out the stock to applying the finish, is detailed with a captioned color photograph.

| | | |
|---|---|---|
| Size: 8 1/2" x 11" | step-by-step photographs | 96 pp. |
| ISBN: 0-88740-588-6 | soft cover | $18.95 |

**Classic Carved Furniture: Making a Piecrust Tea Table** Tom Heller and Ron Clarkson, *text written with and photography by Douglas Congdon-Martin.* One of the most desirable pieces of American furniture, this tilting top table has the high elegance of eighteenth century design. Finely carved throughout, it brings together the skills of furniture maker and carver. Every step, from cutting and turning to carving and finishing, is explained in step-by-step photographs.

| | | |
|---|---|---|
| Size: 8 1/2" x 11" | 500 color & b-w photos | 128 pp. |
| ISBN: 0-88740-616-5 | $19.95 | |

**Step-by-step to a Classic Fireplace Mantel** Steve Penberthy with Gary Jones, *text written with and photograpy by Douglas Congdon-Martin.* Build a classic mantel from stock materials and moldings, and tools found in the most basic of workshops. From measurement to the finished product, the authors take the reader through the complete process. Every step is illustrated with a color photograph and a concise instruction. In the back are photographs of many design variations that can be made using the same building techniques. This is, without a doubt, the best book ever published on building mantels and will be a welcome addition to the woodworker's library.

| | | |
|---|---|---|
| Size: 8 1/2" x 11" | 200 color photos + line drawings | 64 pp. |
| ISBN: 0-88740-653-X | soft cover | $12.95 |

Schiffer books may be ordered from your local bookstore, or they may be ordered directly from the publisher by writing to:

Schiffer Publishing, Ltd.
4880 Lower Valley Rd
Atglen PA 19310
(610) 593-1777; Fax (610) 593-2002
E-mail: schifferbk@aol.com

Please include $3.95 for shipping and handling for the first two books and 50¢ for each additional book. Free shipping for orders $100 or more.

Write for a free catalog.
Printed in China